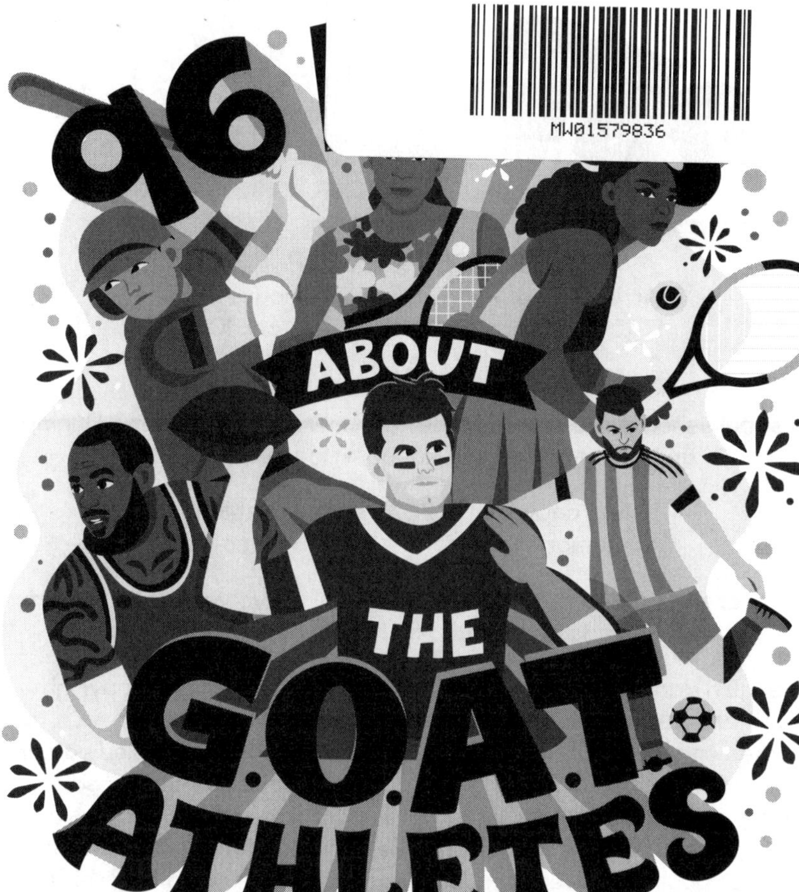

96

ABOUT

THE G.O.A.T. ATHLETES

GREATEST OF ALL TIME

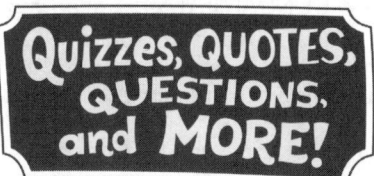

Quizzes, QUOTES, QUESTIONS, and MORE!

BY ARIE KAPLAN

ILLUSTRATED BY Risa Rodil

Grosset & Dunlap

GROSSET & DUNLAP
An imprint of Penguin Random House LLC
1745 Broadway, New York, New York 10019

First published in the United States of America by Grosset & Dunlap,
an imprint of Penguin Random House LLC, 2025

GROSSET & DUNLAP is a registered trademark of
Penguin Random House LLC.

Visit us online at penguinrandomhouse.com.

Manufactured in Canada

ISBN 9780593889008   10 9 8 7 6 5 4 3 2 1 FRI

Design by Kimberley Sampson

TABLE OF CONTENTS

Introduction

Part I

Part II

Part III

Part IV

Part V

INTRODUCTION

Some of the Greatest

This is a book of facts about some of the greatest athletes of all time. *Some* of them. Not *all* of them. The history of organized professional team sports is too rich, too vast, too massive to include *every* great athlete who ever got their hands on a basketball or a baseball bat. That would be . . . a *much* thicker book. This book is just what it appears to be: a curated, subjective list of some of the best people to ever play their respective sports.

But you can be sure of one thing: All of the people in this book are heroes, role models, trailblazers, and pioneers. They're people who did the hard work and did it long enough to see it pay off. Folks that valued courage, discipline, focus, and perseverance, and were willing to go that extra mile. Hopefully, this book will encourage and inspire you to read and learn more about some of the *other* great athletes out there. And it might inspire *you* to go the extra mile in your own life as well. Hey, you never know. Maybe *you're* the next great athlete. The world just doesn't know it yet.

Part 1

HOOP HEROES: BASKETBALL

Michael Jordan

Michael Jordan's signature style is unmistakable: his wagging tongue; his fleet-footed, somewhat theatrical maneuvers; and his legendary leaping ability. Those moves are why people call him "Air Jordan."

Michael was drafted by the Chicago Bulls in 1984. For his first few seasons with the Bulls, he definitely distinguished himself, but he did not have a National Basketball Association (NBA) title on his résumé. This changed in 1991, when Michael led the Bulls to the championship, a feat he also repeated in 1992 and 1993.

After a brief detour into the world of professional baseball in 1993, Michael returned to the Bulls two years later. He then repeated his earlier "three-peat," as the Jordan-led Bulls once again won three consecutive championships between 1996 and 1998. And this is why Michael Jordan is considered a legend.

FREE THROW FACTS!

Michael Jordan was born in Brooklyn, New York, on February 17, 1963.

But when Michael was young, his family moved to Wilmington, North Carolina, which is where he grew up.

LeBron James

Many consider LeBron James one of the greatest all-around basketball players ever to dunk a ball. As of this writing, he has won four NBA championships across three different teams: the Cleveland Cavaliers, the Miami Heat, and his current team, the Los Angeles Lakers.

LeBron was first drafted by the Cavaliers in 2003. After seven years with the Cavs, he signed with the Miami Heat. But after he'd been with the Heat for a while, something ate at him: He'd never won a championship in Cleveland. And he missed his home state of Ohio.

So in 2014, he returned to the Cavaliers. Then during the 2015–2016 season, LeBron led the Cavs back from the brink of defeat, and by game seven, they won their first championship in the history of the franchise.

Today, LeBron is still working hard, still excelling. In 2023, he became the all-time leading scorer in NBA history, showing why fans call him "King James."

FREE THROW FACTS!

LeBron James was born on December 30, 1984, in Akron, Ohio.

When LeBron signed with the Miami Heat in 2010, this caused some controversy, because fans in Cleveland were upset that he was leaving.

Kobe Bryant

Kobe Bryant spent a good chunk of his childhood in Italy, so when he came back to the United States at age thirteen, he felt like he didn't fit in. Kobe worked out his frustrations on the basketball court, sharpening his skills. And he got so good that he was drafted straight from high school into the NBA in 1996. It taught him that great preparation leads to great success.

Kobe learned the same lesson after his first difficult season with the Los Angeles Lakers. He spent the next couple of seasons training, working, and improving. And in his fourth season, Kobe—alongside Shaquille O'Neal—led the Lakers to the 2000 NBA title.

By the time Kobe retired in 2016, he was a five-time winner of the NBA Championship. And although he lost his life in a helicopter crash in 2020, Kobe's legacy remains. He'll always be remembered as one of the best and most hardworking players in basketball history.

FREE THROW FACTS!

Kobe Bryant was born on August 23, 1978, in Philadelphia, Pennsylvania.

Kobe's dad, Joe Bryant, was also a professional basketball player.

Diana Taurasi

Diana Taurasi has said that her fighting spirit—her competitive edge—is what separates her from your average, garden-variety basketball player. And she's right. Over the past two decades, Diana has racked up a truly dizzying list of accomplishments.

In 2004, she was drafted by the Phoenix Mercury. Three years later, thanks in part to Diana's skill and tenacity, the Mercury advanced to the Women's National Basketball Association (WNBA) finals, eventually winning the team's first championship. As of this writing, she's won two other WNBA championships (in 2009 and 2014), as well as five Olympic gold medals.

In 2021, she led the Mercury back to the finals, but this time they *lost* the championship. However, there was a silver lining: At the start of those finals, Diana was voted *the greatest WNBA player of all time*.

FREE THROW FACTS!

Diana Taurasi was born on June 11, 1982, in Glendale, California.

In 2009, Diana was named the league's MVP (Most Valuable Player).

Slam-Dunk Stats

1 Before being drafted by the Bulls, Michael Jordan enrolled at the University of North Carolina in 1981, and quickly became a rising star in the university's basketball team.

2 During the 1986–1987 season, Michael Jordan became only the second basketball player—after Wilt Chamberlain—to score more than three thousand points in a single season.

3 From 2001 to 2003, Michael played for the Washington Wizards.

4 Throughout his high school basketball career, LeBron James led his team at Akron's St. Vincent-St. Mary Catholic High School to win three state titles.

5 When LeBron was three years old, his mother, Gloria, bought him a kid-size basketball and hoop set as a Christmas gift.

6 Three-year-old LeBron had no problem reaching the hoop and making a slam dunk, even when the hoop was raised as high as it could go.

7 Kobe Bryant's dad, Joe, played basketball for the 76ers.

8 When Kobe was little, he loved to watch his dad play basketball on TV.

9 Diana Taurasi is the first player in the history of the WNBA to have reached 10,000 career points, 1,500 rebounds, and 1,500 assists.

10 Diana became the all-time leading scorer for WNBA finals shots in 2014.

What You Do

"If you really want to do something different than everyone else, then you have to do things that are different."

—Diana Taurasi on carving your own path in life

Is there something that you do differently than everyone else? What is that thing? Is it playing basketball? Playing another sport? Writing? Drawing? Solving math problems? Dancing? Write about that "something"—and how you do it differently—on the lines below.

_____

_____

_____

_____

_____

_____

_____

_____

_____

_____

_____

_____

_____

_____

_____

_____

_____

_____

Cartoons and You!

In the 1996 movie *Space Jam*, Michael Jordan goes on an adventure with Bugs Bunny and his cartoon friends. If you went on an adventure with your favorite cartoon characters, what would that adventure be like? Write about it on the lines below.

_____

_____

_____

_____

_____

_____

_____

_____

_____

_____

_____

_____

_____

_____

_____

_____

_____

_____

"Postgame Puzzlers" Quiz

1) Michael Jordan retired permanently from professional basketball in the year ____.

   a. 2003
   b. 1884
   c. 1610
   d. 1718

2) In 2016, LeBron James played himself in an episode of which children's animated television series?

   a. *Scooby-Doo, Where Are You!*
   b. *The 13 Ghosts of Scooby-Doo*
   c. *Teen Titans Go!*
   d. *A Pup Named Scooby-Doo*

3) Kobe Bryant is named after ____.

   a. Bryant the Bearded, a Viking warrior
   b. Kobe, a type of Japanese beef
   c. Bryant the Brave, a medieval archer
   d. Bryant the Brilliant, an ancient scholar

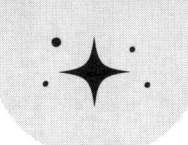

4) Diana Taurasi's father is a professional
   ____ player.

   a. Mandolin
   b. Flute
   c. Guitar
   d. Soccer

5) In 2005, LeBron James broke a record,
   becoming the youngest player (at the
   time) to score over fifty ____ in a game.

   a. Jars of olive oil
   b. Points
   c. Jars of canola oil
   d. Jars of sunflower oil

Check your answers on page 78!

Part II

SUPER SLUGGERS: BASEBALL

Babe Ruth

George Herman "Babe" Ruth Jr. was perhaps the first true celebrity in the history of baseball. Babe was also the most reliable and gifted power-hitter of his era.

In 1920, after the Boston Red Sox sold Babe's contract to the New York Yankees, his prolific slugging upgraded the Yankees from a second-class team to a popular franchise. Attendance rates doubled, and this necessitated the building of Yankee Stadium, also known as "The House That Ruth Built," for the much larger crowds.

During his career, Babe notched an incredible 714 home runs. And that's to say nothing of his seven World Series championships (three with the Red Sox and four with the Yankees). But more importantly, thanks to his natural talent, flamboyant style, and ability to draw a crowd, Babe established baseball as America's pastime.

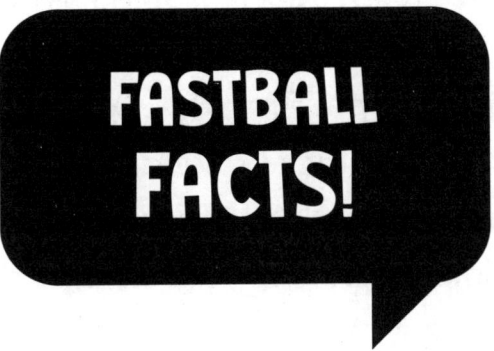

FASTBALL FACTS!

Babe Ruth was born on February 6, 1895, in Baltimore, Maryland.

Babe hit the first home run ever inside Yankee Stadium.

Jackie Robinson

On April 15, 1947, Jackie Robinson changed history when he broke the so-called "color line" by playing for the Brooklyn Dodgers and becoming the first Black baseball player to play Major League Baseball (MLB) in the United States. The importance of this cannot be overstated.

From the beginning of his career with the Dodgers, Jackie faced racist insults, sometimes from the crowds and sometimes from his fellow players. But he maintained a core of inner strength, ignoring the jeers and concentrating on building a stellar career. With that in mind, in 1947, the same year he joined the Dodgers, Jackie was named Rookie of the Year. Two years later, he was named National League MVP.

During an MLB career that lasted a mere nine years, Jackie led the Dodgers to six league championships and one World Series win.

FASTBALL FACTS!

Jackie Robinson was born on January 31, 1919, in Cairo, Georgia.

Thanks to Jackie Robinson breaking the "color line" in 1947, other Black players like Willie Mays and Hank Aaron signed MLB contracts in the years that followed.

Aaron Judge

Aaron Judge knows what it's like to work your way to the top. He began in the minor leagues, showing much promise. Then, in August and September 2016, during the first couple of months of his Major League career playing for the New York Yankees, he started out strong but eventually struggled. His batting average plummeted.

By his first full season with the Yankees in early 2017, he had vastly improved. Aaron began the season as Rookie of the Month and ended it with fifty-two home runs, a new record for a rookie. But that's not all! Thirty-three of those homers were at Yankee Stadium. This shattered the record previously held by Babe Ruth for most home runs hit in Yankee home games.

Then in the fall of 2022, Aaron smashed the American League record for single-season home runs set by Roger Maris in 1961. Roger had hit sixty-one homers. Aaron hit sixty-two.

FASTBALL FACTS!

Aaron Judge was born on April 26, 1992, and grew up in Linden, California.

"All Rise" is what a bailiff says when a judge enters a courtroom, to indicate that people should stand up. And because Aaron's last name is "Judge," his nickname is "All Rise."

Shohei Ohtani

Shohei Ohtani is unique because he is equally gifted at both hitting and pitching. This is called being a "two-way" player.

When Shohei started playing for the Los Angeles Angels in early 2018, he pitched, and he *also* batted as the designated hitter during his off days from pitching. That made him a *full-time* two-way MLB player, the first of his kind in nearly a century.

Shohei's effectiveness as both a starting pitcher and a designated hitter really resonates with fans. In 2022, he achieved a historic first for the World Series era, becoming the first player in this era to be eligible for the leaderboards as both a pitcher and a hitter . . . in the *same* year.

At the end of 2023, Shohei announced that he had left the Angels and signed with the Los Angeles Dodgers, doubling Dodgers ticket prices. Some call this spike in ticket sales "the Shohei Ohtani Effect."

FASTBALL FACTS!

Shohei Ohtani was born on July 5, 1994, in Oshu, Japan.

The "World Series era" is the current era, which began in 1903.

Home-Run History

1 In 1914, Babe Ruth signed with the Baltimore Orioles.

2 Back then, the Orioles were a minor league team.

3 George Herman Ruth Jr. first picked up the nickname "Babe" when he was playing for the Orioles.

4 Jackie Robinson was inducted into the National Baseball Hall of Fame in 1962.

5 In 1963, Jackie Robinson marched on Washington with Dr. Martin Luther King Jr.

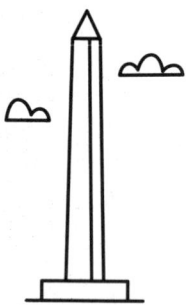

6 Every year since 2004, Major League Baseball has celebrated Jackie's accomplishments and legacy on April 15, which is known as Jackie Robinson Day.

7 Aaron Judge keeps the number ".179" on his cell phone. That's the lowest his batting average was, back when it had plummeted in 2016.

8 Aaron keeps it on his cell phone so he'll remember the times when he was struggling.

9 Before Shohei Ohtani, the last full-time two-way player of any real significance in Major League Baseball was Babe Ruth.

10 For this reason, Shohei has sometimes been compared to Babe Ruth.

New Experiences

"It's a new country, new professional life. There's a lot to be nervous about."

—Shohei Ohtani on how he felt about coming to America to play baseball

Has there ever been a time when you've had to do something for the first time? Did it make you nervous? Did any of your friends or family members help you feel better? Write about it on the lines below.

_____

_____

_____

_____

_____

_____

_____

_____

_____

_____

_____

_____

_____

_____

_____

_____

_____

_____

_____

_____

_____

A Movie About You!

In 1950, Jackie Robinson played himself in a movie called *The Jackie Robinson Story*. If a movie studio was making a film about you, would you want to play yourself? Or would you want a movie star to play you? And if you could cast a movie star to play you, who would you get? Write about it on the lines below.

_____

_____

_____

_____

_____

_____

_____

_____

_____

_____

_____

_____

_____

_____

_____

_____

_____

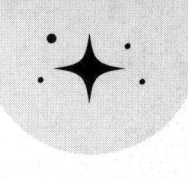

"Postgame Puzzlers" Quiz

1) Aside from "Babe," George Herman Ruth Jr. had other nicknames, including ____.

   a. Spider-Man
   b. The Sultan of Swat
   c. Doctor Strange
   d. Iron Man

2) **Where did Jackie Robinson attend college in 1939?**

   a. University of California Los Angeles (UCLA)
   b. New York University
   c. New York City College of Technology
   d. New York Institute of Art and Design

3) **Because of Aaron Judge's popularity, the Yankees set up a special row of seats in right field called "Judge's Chambers," where Aaron Judge fans can dress up in ____.**

   a. Astronaut outfits
   b. Cowboy hats
   c. Black judge's robes
   d. Superhero costumes

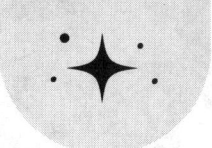

4) In his native country, Japan, where he played baseball before he came to the United States, Shohei Ohtani served as both the pitcher and the designated ____ for the Nippon Ham Fighters.

a. Cool guy
b. Cool dude
c. Cool baseball guy
d. Hitter

5) When Shohei was playing with the Los Angeles Angels, he was friends with Angels center ____ Mike Trout.

a. Vampire
b. Werewolf
c. Fielder
d. Mummy

Check your answers on page 78!

Part III

GRIDIRON GREATS: FOOTBALL

Jim Brown

A three-time MVP, Jim Brown is often considered one of the greatest running backs in American football history.

Playing for the Cleveland Browns for a mere nine seasons—from 1957 to 1965—he led the National Football League (NFL) in rushing for each of those years except for 1962. In just those nine years, Jim scored 126 career touchdowns in only 118 career games. And he led the Browns to the NFL championship three times, winning the title in 1964.

Famous for his energetic and evasive running style, Jim ran for at least 100 yards in 58 of his 118 regular-season games. In 2002, the Sporting News dubbed Jim Brown the greatest football player ever.

FUMBLE FACTS!

Jim Brown was born on February 17, 1936, on St. Simons Island, which is located off the southern coast of Georgia.

In addition to being a football star, Jim Brown was also a civil rights activist, and he formed groups to help Black-owned businesses.

Joe Montana

Joe Montana led the San Francisco 49ers to four Super Bowl championships throughout his time with that team, earning three Super Bowl MVP Awards.

Famously, in 1989, during Joe's third Super Bowl, it looked like all hope was lost and the 49ers would lose to the Cincinnati Bengals. But Joe kept a cool head and with steely resolve, he drove his offense ninety-two yards, passing the winning touchdown with less than sixty seconds left to play.

However, even though Joe had taken the 49ers to their loftiest heights and helped to make them the preeminent NFL team of the 1980s, he was traded to the Kansas City Chiefs in 1993. After two solid seasons with the Chiefs, he retired in 1995, and today he's often thought of as one of the greatest quarterbacks of all time.

FUMBLE FACTS!

Joe Montana was born on June 11, 1956, in New Eagle, Pennsylvania.

Because he's known for keeping a level head under great pressure, Joe Montana earned the nickname "Joe Cool."

Tom Brady

Initially a baseball player who was drafted by the Montreal Expos, Tom Brady changed course early on and decided to play football instead. In 2000, he was drafted by the New England Patriots, and this kicked off an impressive twenty-year career with the team, followed by a three-year run with the Tampa Bay Buccaneers. Turns out baseball's loss is football's gain!

In total, Tom has won seven Super Bowl championships, which is an NFL record. He was also named the game's MVP five times.

During the 2017 Super Bowl, Tom led the Patriots in their triumph over the Atlanta Falcons. And it was a historic victory because it was a huge comeback for the Patriots.

FUMBLE FACTS!

Tom Brady was born on August 3, 1977, in San Mateo, California.

As a child, Tom Brady idolized Joe Montana.

Travis Kelce

A tight end for the Kansas City Chiefs, Travis Kelce has helped his team win three Super Bowls (in 2020, 2023, and 2024).

He's known to go the extra mile. Or in this case, the extra yard. That's because, in each season from 2016 to 2022, Travis racked up over one thousand receiving yards, a record for a tight end.

At the 2024 Super Bowl, Travis contributed nine catches for a total of ninety-three yards. The Chiefs won, triumphing over the San Francisco 49ers.

FUMBLE FACTS!

Travis Kelce was born on October 5, 1989, in Westlake, Ohio.

In reporting on the 2024 Super Bowl, a journalist at ESPN.com said that Travis might be the best tight end in the history of football.

Touchdown Tidbits

1 Before Jim Brown played for the Cleveland Browns, he went to Syracuse University, where he played football, basketball, and lacrosse, and ran track.

2 After he retired from his football career, Jim Brown became an actor, and some consider him to be the first Black action star.

3 That's because many of the films Jim made were action-adventure movies, and few Black actors before him appeared in action films.

4 Joe Montana made his NFL debut on September 16, 1979.

5 Joe was voted first-team All-Pro in 1987, 1989, and 1990.

6 That means he was chosen as one of the best players in the NFL.

7 Before he retired, Tom Brady was known for studying game film (video footage from previous games).

8 Tom did this in order to look for an advantage that would help him and his team in the future.

9 At the 2023 Super Bowl, Travis Kelce went up against his own brother, Jason Kelce, a center for the Philadelphia Eagles.

10 It was the first time the siblings faced off in the Super Bowl.

Goal-Oriented

"It's fun to put goals up on the board and say, 'I want to do this. I want to do this.'"

—Travis Kelce on the importance of setting goals for yourself

Do you like to set goals for yourself? Is there a time that setting a goal—envisioning something you want to do—helped you out? How did you go about making it happen? What steps did you take? If you've never set a goal for anything, is that something you'd like to do? Write about it on the lines below.

_____

_____

_____

_____

_____

_____

_____

_____

_____

_____

_____

_____

_____

_____

_____

_____

_____

_____

_____

That's What Friends Are For

In 1967, Jim Brown organized a meeting of prominent Black athletes to show their support for their friend, heavyweight boxer Muhammad Ali. Can you think of a time when one of your friends was there for you, to show you support in a difficult situation? Or was there a time when *you* did something to show your support for one of your friends? Write about it on the lines below.

_____

_____

_____

_____

_____

_____

_____

_____

_____

_____

_____

_____

_____

_____

_____

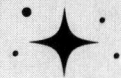

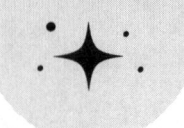

"Postgame Puzzlers" Quiz

1) In 1971, Jim Brown was inducted into the Pro Football Hall of ____.

    a. Mirrors
    b. Fun House Mirrors
    c. Fame
    d. Mirrored Disco Balls

2) Jim Brown's film acting credits include the 1967 war movie *The Dirty Dozen* and the 1996 alien invasion film ____.

    a. *Mr. Smith Goes to Washington*
    b. *Mars Attacks!*
    c. *Mr. Deeds Goes to Town*
    d. *Mr. and Mrs. Smith*

3) Joe Montana attended ____ from 1975 to 1979.

    a. Clown College
    b. Mime School
    c. Harlequin Academy
    d. The University of Notre Dame

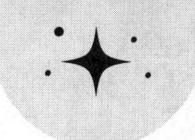

4) Tom Brady is the first quarterback to win seven ____.

    a. French fries
    b. Loaves of french bread
    c. Super Bowls
    d. Pieces of french toast

5) Travis Kelce selected eighty-seven as his uniform number because his ____ was born in 1987.

    a. Favorite owl
    b. Favorite sparrow
    c. Favorite crow
    d. Brother Jason

Check your answers on page 78!

Part IV

CLEATS AND COURAGE: SOCCER

Mia Hamm

A disciplined athlete who is widely respected for her speed, skill, and goal-scoring talent, Mia Hamm won the Women's World Cup in 1991, when she was nineteen years old. Mia won the Women's World Cup again in 1999, and she took home gold medals at the Olympics in 1996 and 2004.

For two consecutive years, in 2001 and 2002, Mia was named Women's World Player of the Year by the Fédération Internationale de Football Association (FIFA).

By the time she retired from the national team in 2004, Mia had notched 158 goals in international competition, which (at the time) was the most by any player.

FREE KICK FACTS!

Mia was born Mariel Margaret Hamm on March 17, 1972, in Selma, Alabama.

Mia's record of 158 goals was broken in 2013 by Abby Wambach.

Cristiano Ronaldo

In 2003, eighteen-year-old Portuguese soccer prodigy Cristiano Ronaldo signed with Manchester United—or "Man U" for short—and was instantly recognized as a dazzling young forward.

In 2008, during a tense nail-biter of a game, Cristiano helped Man U win a Champions League trophy. That year, he won a Ballon d'Or ("Golden Ball") as the world's top player.

Around that time, he left Man U and signed with Real Madrid, which is another soccer club. (In some parts of the world, people say "club" instead of "team.") Cristiano would play with different clubs over the next several years, including coming back to Man U in 2021.

FREE KICK FACTS!

Cristiano Ronaldo dos Santos Aveiro was born on February 5, 1985, on the island of Madeira, which is roughly six hundred miles off the coast of Portugal.

But make no mistake—Madeira is a region of Portugal, and Cristiano is a proud Portuguese citizen!

Lionel Messi

Argentine soccer star Lionel "Leo" Messi made his debut at age seventeen in 2004 playing for FC Barcelona. He quickly established himself as a quick, effective pass distributor who could maneuver his way through a densely packed defense.

By 2008, after years of hard work and training, Lionel was one of the most acclaimed soccer players in the world, often mentioned in the same breath as Cristiano Ronaldo.

Lionel led Argentina to the World Cup final in 2014 . . . but Argentina lost. However, there was a silver lining: Lionel won the Ballon d'Or as the best player in the tournament!

FREE KICK FACTS!

Lionel Messi was born on June 24, 1987, in Rosario, Argentina.

In 2021 and 2022 respectively, Lionel led Argentina's national team to win the Copa América and World Cup.

Megan Rapinoe

Megan Rapinoe has said that she thinks of each soccer match as a stage, and she thinks of herself as a performer who's "trying to entertain." And the famous 2019 photo of her with her arms outstretched—in what many people call her power pose—is certainly theatrical.

But for some, that photo also sends a serious message, because it represents women's refusal to retreat in the face of adversity. You see, the photo was taken at the 2019 Women's World Cup, where Megan won her second gold medal.

Also in 2019, she won the Ballon d'Or Féminin and The Best FIFA Women's Player award.

Over the years, Megan has inspired many people with her athletic career as well as her activism on behalf of the LGBTQIA+ community.

FREE KICK FACTS!

Megan Rapinoe was born on July 5, 1985, in Redding, California.

Megan won her *first* Women's World Cup gold medal in 2015.

Kickoff Knowledge

1 In many parts of the world, the sport Americans call "soccer" is known as "football" or "fútbol."

2 Mia Hamm began playing competitively when she was a teenager.

3 From 2001 to 2003, Mia played for the Washington Freedom, a team which (at the time) was owned by the short-lived Women's United Soccer Association.

4 In 2021, Cristiano Ronaldo scored a very important goal—his 110th, which shattered the existing record.

5 This made Cristiano the all-time leading male international scorer.

6 At the end of 2022, Cristiano left Man U and signed with the Saudi Arabian soccer club Al Nassr.

7 On May 1, 2005, Lionel Messi became the youngest player in history to score a goal for FC Barcelona.

8 He was seventeen years old at the time.

9 Megan Rapinoe retired from the world of professional soccer in late 2023.

10 According to CNN.com, when Megan Rapinoe won The Best award from FIFA in 2019, this confirmed that she was the greatest women's soccer player in the world at that time.

Dreams Come True

"I grew up on the Olympics, and the opportunity to win a gold medal was a dream come true."

—Mia Hamm on watching her dreams become reality

Do you ever think about what you want to do for a living when you become an adult? What would your dream job be? Write about it on the lines below.

_____

_____

_____

_____

_____

_____

_____

_____

_____

_____

_____

_____

_____

_____

_____

_____

_____

_____

_____

_____

_____

_____

_____

"Postgame Puzzlers" Quiz

1) Mia Hamm won a ____ medal at the 2000 Olympics.

    a. Silver
    b. Licorice
    c. Chocolate
    d. Marshmallow

2) Cristiano Ronaldo grew up in ____, the biggest city on the island of Madeira.

    a. Big City
    b. Large City
    c. Massive City
    d. Funchal

3) Lionel Messi's older brother Rodrigo nicknamed him the ____.

    a. Income Tax Attorney
    b. Flea
    c. Certified Public Accountant
    d. Tech Company CEO

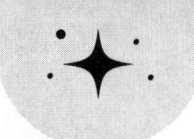

4) Megan Rapinoe competed in the 2016 Olympics, which were held in ____.

a. Brazil
b. Loompaland
c. The Smurf Village
d. The planet Arrakis

5) Megan was named one of _____ magazine's Most Influential People in 2020.

a. *Fly-Fishing*
b. *Kite Fishing*
c. *Freshwater Fishing*
d. *Time*

Check your answers on page 78!

Part V

CHAMPIONS OF THE COURT: TENNIS

Arthur Ashe

A cerebral, graceful player who could send tennis balls careening past his opponents like meteors, Arthur Ashe was the first African American to play on the United States Davis Cup team, in 1963.

Arthur came of age in the 1950s, when Black people and white people in America were segregated, or separated. But as Arthur's career began, things were starting to change. So he made a lot of historic "firsts." It took great courage to do this.

In 1968, he was the first Black man to win the US Open, and in 1975, he was the first Black man to win Wimbledon.

In 1993, Arthur Ashe died of AIDS-related pneumonia at age forty-nine. But his legacy—as a tennis player who was an expert strategist, and as a person of exceptional bravery—remains.

FOREHAND FACTS!

Arthur Ashe was born on July 10, 1943, in Richmond, Virginia.

Arthur helped the United States win three championships, in 1968, 1969, and 1970.

Serena and Venus Williams

Serena Williams revitalized women's tennis. But she didn't do it alone. Serena and her sister Venus forever altered the sport with their unique play style. Before they came on the scene, most players would simply try to hit the ball to a place where their opponents couldn't hit it. But the Williams sisters brought a power to their serves that few others did.

Throughout the course of their careers, Venus and Serena teamed up to win a total of fourteen Grand Slam doubles titles. And at the Olympics, the two went home with three doubles gold medals (in 2000, 2008, and 2012).

But they don't always work together. In 2017, Serena won the Australian Open, setting a new record by winning twenty-three Grand Slam singles titles in the open era, more than anyone else (at that time).

FOREHAND FACTS!

Venus Williams was born on June 17, 1980, in Lynwood, California.

Serena Williams was born on September 26, 1981, in Saginaw, Michigan.

Roger Federer

Prone to inventive shot-making techniques and possessed of a fluid forehand, Roger Federer helped bring professional tennis to new heights of popularity in the early twenty-first century with his charisma and fancy footwork.

In the 2000s and 2010s, few would argue that Roger wasn't one of the best players in tennis. Every year from 2004 to 2008, he won the US Open. In 2017, Roger won his eighth Wimbledon title, breaking the previous record. The following year, he won his twentieth Grand Slam singles championship, setting a new record for *that* tournament.

And although he announced his retirement in late 2022, Roger has been busy ever since with philanthropic projects designed to help children in need.

FOREHAND FACTS!

Roger Federer was born on August 8, 1981, in Basel, Switzerland.

At the end of 2004, Roger was ranked as the number one tennis player in the world.

Coco Gauff

From the time she was a small child, Cori Dionne "Coco" Gauff wanted to be the greatest tennis player on Earth. For this reason, Coco's whole family moved from their home in Atlanta, Georgia, to Delray Beach, Florida, so that Coco could train at one of the high-quality tennis training camps located in Delray Beach.

When Coco was fifteen years old, she defeated her childhood hero Venus Williams at Wimbledon in July 2019. As usual, Coco was cool under pressure during the tournament, which has come to be one of her hallmarks.

Four years later, in 2023, a nineteen-year-old Coco won the US Open women's title, making her only the third American teenager to ever have won the national women's title.

FOREHAND FACTS!

Coco Gauff was born on March 13, 2004, in Delray Beach, Florida.

When Coco was ten years old, she trained with Patrick Mouratoglou, who is Serena Williams's former coach.

Match-Point Memories

1 When Arthur Ashe won Wimbledon in 1975, he defeated Jimmy Connors, who was—until then—the number one tennis player in the world.

2 In 1978, Arthur won the Pacific Southwest Open.

3 In 1980, Arthur retired from tennis, and worked as an activist and humanitarian.

4 At the Lipton Championship tennis tournament in 1999, Venus faced off against Serena.

5 It was the first time since 1884 that two sisters were opponents in a major professional tennis tournament!

6 In 2015, Serena Williams was named *Sports Illustrated*'s Sportsperson of the Year.

7 Roger Federer won a silver medal at the 2012 Olympic Games in London, England.

8 In 2006, Roger competed in seventeen tournaments, reaching the finals in sixteen of them and winning twelve.

9 Coco Gauff's real name is Cori, and she's named after her father, Corey.

10 But because the names "Cori" and "Corey" sound so similar, Cori's aunt suggested that she adopt the nickname "Coco" to avoid confusion.

ANSWER KEY

Pages 20–21:
1) a, 2) c, 3) b, 4) d, 5) b

Pages 36–37:
1) b, 2) a, 3) c, 4) d, 5) c

Pages 52–53:
1) c, 2) b, 3) d, 4) c, 5) d

Pages 66–67:
1) a, 2) d, 3) b, 4) a, 5) d

ABOUT THE AUTHOR

Arie Kaplan was born and raised in Baltimore, Maryland, which is absolutely the only thing he has in common with Babe Ruth. Arie wrote the six-volume ShockZone: Games and Gamers series of children's nonfiction books, which covered every aspect of the video game industry. He also wrote the award-winning nonfiction title *From Krakow to Krypton: Jews and Comic Books*, which was a finalist for the National Jewish Book Award.

Aside from his work as a nonfiction author, Arie has written numerous books and graphic novels for young readers, including *Jurassic Park Little Golden Book*, *Frankie and the Dragon*, *LEGO Star Wars: The Official Stormtrooper Training Manual*, *The New Kid from Planet Glorf*, *Batman: Harley at Bat!*, *Spider-Man Comictivity*, *Shadow Guy and Gamma Gal: Heroes Unite*, and *Speed Racer: Chronicles of the Racer*. In addition, Arie is a screenwriter for television, video games, and transmedia. Please check out his website: www.ariekaplan.com.